The Quick and Dirty Introduction to Software Configuration Management

Lloyd Kaufman

The Quick and Dirty Introduction to Software Configuration Management

Lloyd Kaufman

ISBN 978-1-7777210-3-9

Bootstrap IT

A division of DBC Technology Services Inc.

bootstrap-it.com

office@bootstrap-it.com

Contents

An Introduction to Software Configuration Management

Let's begin by defining some related terms.

Configuration management is the process of managing and controlling changes to the configuration of a system. Configuration management includes the identification of changes, the recording of changes, and the approval or rejection of changes.

Software Configuration Management (SCM) is the process of managing changes to software. This includes identifying changes, tracking changes, and managing the distribution of software updates. SCM helps organizations ensure that their software is reliable and consistent.

Infrastructure as Code (IaC) is the process of managing and provisioning compute, network and storage resources using software-defined models. IaC tools allow you to manage your infrastructure through code, similar to the way you write code for applications. This approach enables you to version control your infrastructure, automate its deployment and scaling, and audit changes.

Configuration automation is the process of automatically configuring devices using software. This can include automatically installing software, configuring devices, and setting up services. Configuration automation can help reduce the amount of time needed to configure devices, and can help ensure that devices are configured correctly.

Continuous configuration automation is the process of automating the management and configuration of servers, networking devices, and applications. Continuous configuration automation typically employs software that enables administrators to automatically deploy new server instances, configure networking devices, and install and configure applications.

Continuous Configuration Automation is most effective when it is used to manage the configuration of systems that are under frequent change.

It's hard to go wrong with this kind of automation. The trick, however, is figuring out which automation tools to use and then how to integrate them into your infrastructure and workflow in a way that doesn't cause too much short-term pain. That'll be our goal for the rest of this book.

It'll be helpful to start things rolling by talking about some important models used by various SCM tools.

Declarative vs. imperative

The *declarative* model is one approach to configuration automation that relies on a set of defined rules to determine how devices should be configured. In this model, devices are described in terms of their desired configuration, and a tool or process uses these descriptions to automatically configure the devices. This approach is often used to manage large numbers of devices or systems, and it helps ensure that all devices are configured in a consistent manner.

Imperative automation (sometimes referred to as *procedural*) is a model of configuration automation in which a set of instructions, or commands, are executed *in a specific order* to achieve a desired outcome. This model is typically used to manage tasks or processes that are difficult or time-consuming to complete manually.

The imperative model of configuration automation consists of three main components: commands, modules, and tasks. Commands are the basic building blocks of the imperative model. They are used to initiate actions and perform operations on modules. Modules are self-contained units of code that contain one or more commands. They can be used to group related commands together, making them easier to manage and maintain. Tasks are collections of modules that represent specific actions or processes. They can be used to automate complex workflows or repeatable tasks.

The imperative model of configuration automation is based on a sequence of commands that must be executed in a specific order in order to achieve a desired outcome. This sequence can be represented as a flowchart diagram that shows the individual steps necessary to complete the task at hand. The flowchart can also be used as a blueprint for creating automated scripts that will execute the same sequence of commands automatically.

Push vs. pull

The push model of configuration automation refers to the deployment of updates and changes to a system automatically, without any user input. This is typically done through the use of scripts or other automated tools that are run on a regular basis.

The pull model, on the other hand, refers to the manual retrieval of updates and changes from a centralized location by individual users or systems. This model relies on users being aware of changes that have been made and then taking the necessary steps to download and install those changes themselves.

Idempotency

Idempotency is the principle that a configuration change should only be made once, and that it should be made in such a way that if it is made more than once, the end result is the same as if it had been made only once. In other words, the principle of idempotency says that it is safe to run a configuration change script multiple times.

State management

In configuration automation, state management is the process of managing the configuration of devices, systems, or applications. Configuration management software is used to track and manage changes to the system's configuration. State management can help ensure that devices are configured in a consistent manner and that changes are tracked and documented.

Software Configuration Management Tools

For all their differences, what all of the tools we'll soon discuss share in common is that they're built to manage the versions and configurations of software products. These tools help to identify and track the changes made to software products, as well as manage the distribution of these products. They also help to ensure that only authorized changes are made to software applications.

For the remainder of this chapter, we'll explore the function, design, and some code examples of:

- Puppet
- Chef
- Ansible
- SaltStack
- Terraform
- Docker
- PowerShell DSC

Let's dive right in.

Puppet

Puppet is built with Ruby and uses a declarative language to describe the desired state of the system. It then uses this description to configure the system accordingly. Such configuration can include installing software, configuring services, and managing users.

In puppet, a *configuration* is a set of instructions that define how a system should look and behave. A puppet configuration typically includes:

- Definitions of the system's components, including classes, modules, and resources
- Configurations for the system's services
- Configurations for the system's users

A Puppet *module* is a collection of files that define a specific piece of functionality. A module can be used to manage a particular type of server, or to provide shared functionality across multiple servers. Modules are written in the Puppet language, and are installed on individual servers using the `puppet apply` command.

Resources are the fundamental building blocks of Puppet. In Puppet, a resource is anything that can be managed. This includes servers, applications, files, and users. Puppet resources can be defined in manifests, or they can be automatically generated by Puppet.

A Puppet *manifest* is a file (saved with a `.pp` extension) that stores information about one or more puppet modules. It includes the name of the module, the version of the module, and a list of the classes contained in the module.

An *agent* is a process that can be controlled by Puppet. It runs on nodes to retrieve configuration manifests from the Puppet server and apply them to the node.

Here is a typical example of a Puppet manifest. This one, designed to run on a Linux distribution in the Debian family, has three tasks:

- Update system software
- Ensure that the "nano" program is installed
- Create a text file called `myfile` in the `/tmp/` directory.

```
exec { 'apt-get update':
    command => '/usr/bin/apt-get update'
}

package { 'nano':
    ensure => 'installed'
    require => Exec['apt-get update']
}
class module1::class1 {
  file { '/tmp/myfile':
    ensure  => 'present',
    content => 'Some simple content',
    path    => '/tmp/myfile',
  }
}
```

As with all the code examples you'll see in this chapter, this manifest file is very simple and uses only a tiny subset of the available features. The goal is only to give you a taste of the tool for comparison purposes.

Progress Chef

Like Puppet, Progress Chef (formally known as "Chef") also works with a server-client architecture and operates using a "pull" model. It's also Ruby-based and generally requires command line setup.

A Chef *server* hosts all cookbooks, node data, and roles. A Chef server can be used to manage multiple Chef nodes. A Chef "node" is a machine that is configured and managed by Chef.

A Chef *resource* is a description of the desired state of your system and of what must happen on the system in order to achieve that state. Multiple resources are combined to form recipes.

In Chef, an *attribute* is a named value that can be assigned to a node, role, or recipe. Attributes can be used to configure nodes, pass data to recipes, or control the execution of recipes. One example of a Chef attribute is `ignore_failure`. This attribute determines whether Chef will continue to run recipes after a failed run.

The Chef client/server mode architecture provides a centralized Chef server that manages all the nodes in your infrastructure. The Chef *server* stores all the data and configuration information for your nodes. The Chef *client* communicates with the Chef server to retrieve this information and to run *knife* commands. Knife is a command-line tool that lets you interact with the Chef server.

```
knife cookbook upload lamp_stack
knife cookbook list
```

Chef-solo mode does not use a central server, instead relying on the local machine for all cookbook storage and management.

A Chef cookbook is a collection of recipes that can be used to manage the configuration of a system or application. The recipes can be used to install software, configure settings, and manage files.

This simple `website.rb` configuration (where the file extension `.rb` tells us that the language is Ruby) does three things:

- Create a file called `hello.text` and write some content to it
- Install the Apache HTTP server package
- Configure Apache to start up immediately and on each subsequent system boot

```
file 'hello.txt' do
  content 'Welcome to Chef'
end
package "apache2" do
  action :install
end

service "apache2" do
  action [:enable, :start]
end
```

You can launch the workload with this `chef-apply` command:

```
sudo chef-apply website.rb
```

Ansible

Ansible is a radically simple IT automation engine that automates cloud provisioning, configuration management, application deployment, intra-service orchestration, and many other IT tasks.

Perhaps its biggest attraction is that it's relatively easy to learn. The YAML syntax used by its playbooks and an intuitive structure combine to deliver a versatile environment with a soft learning curve.

Ansible playbooks are organized into "plays" and "tasks". A play is a collection of tasks that will be executed sequentially. Tasks are the individual actions that will be executed as part of a play.

This example playbook will install and run the Apache HTTP server. It invokes the Debian Apt package manager and *systemd* to perform its tasks. The `hosts` value is the name of a inventory file (`group1` in this case) containing a list of host names. Assuming you've already set passwordless SSH access from your workstation, the tasks will be run on each of those hosts.

```
---

- hosts: group1
  tasks:
  - name: Install Apache2 package
    apt:
      name: apache2
      state: latest
  - name: check Apache2 service status
    service:
      name: apache2
      state: started
```

Running the playbook from the command line is easy:

```
ansible-playbook playbook.yml
```

Ansible doesn't require a master server, as you can control your remote nodes using the SSH protocol. Ansible can use sudo to execute commands as root or another user, if needed.

SaltStack

SaltStack uses a remote execution engine called "salt" to manage systems. This allows administrators to manage large numbers of systems easily and quickly. SaltStack uses a distributed architecture which allows for scalability and high availability. The architecture is composed of three main components: the master, the minion, and the proxy.

The master is responsible for managing the Salt environment and all of the minions. It maintains a list of all minions in the environment and their current state. The master also provides a REST API for communicating with minions and retrieving data from them.

Minions are responsible for executing commands sent to them by the master. They communicate with the master over a secure connection, and they can be located anywhere in the world. Minions run in a stateless mode, so they can be restarted without any loss of data or configuration.

The proxy is used to provide secure communication between the master and minions over an insecure network. The proxy can be located anywhere in the world, and it is responsible for encrypting and decrypting messages between the master and minions.

You can fire up SaltStack - once it's been installed - using:

```
systemctl start salt-master
```

Configure the minion by editing `/etc/salt/minion` to include a directive like this:

```
master: saltmaster.example.com
```

From the command line on the client, send a single command to all minions:

```
salt '*' test.version
```

You can add minion configurations through a formula in an SLS file. This one - within the `/srv/salt/nginx/init.sls:` file - will install the Nginx HTTP server:

```
nginx:
  pkg.installed: []
  service.running:
    - require:
      - pkg: nginx
```

And this command will apply the configuration to all the listening minions:

```
salt '*' state.apply nginx
```

Terraform

Terraform is a software tool that enables you to predictably and efficiently create, manage, and deploy infrastructure. Terraform can manage existing and popular service providers as well as custom in-house solutions.

Terraform is particularly powerful as a cloud-based platform used to create and manage cloud infrastructure. The platform allows users to manage resources in a variety of public cloud providers, including Amazon Web Services, Azure, and Google Cloud Platform.

Terraform stands out from many of the other tools we've been discussing through its immutability. Immutability is the concept of an object (a server configuration, for instance) being unable to be changed after it has been created. In the context of configuration automation, this means that once a configuration has been launched, it cannot be changed. This is desirable because it ensures that the configuration file is always in a known state and that any changes are made deliberately.

Similar to cloud and container workloads in general, Terraform achieves this by deleting running containers or compute instances and rebuilding them using an updated configuration, rather than update an existing instance.

Since Terraform is primarily an orchestration rather than a configuration tool, it's a particularly good fit for container-based workloads like Docker. This is because Docker takes care of much of the environment orchestration within its own definitions.

This simple Terraform `main.tf` configuration file would connect to a preconfigured AWS account and launch a specified AMI image as an EC2 compute instance:

```
terraform {
  required_providers {
    aws = {
      source  = "hashicorp/aws"
      version = "~> 3.27"
    }
  }

  required_version = ">= 0.14.9"
}

provider "aws" {
  profile = "default"
  region  = "us-west-2"
}

resource "aws_instance" "app_server" {
  ami           = "ami-830c94e3"
  instance_type = "t2.micro"

  tags = {
    Name = "ExampleAppServerInstance"
  }
}
```

Docker

At first glance, Docker might not seem a great fit with our collection of configuration management tools. After all, isn't it a lower-level container technology? But there's a lot of overlap, and the larger Docker ecosystem includes functionality that'll help you meet nearly all the primary goals of a configuration management. First, let's understand what Docker is.

Docker is a containerization platform that enables developers to build, ship, and run applications inside containers. Docker containers are lightweight and fast to start, which makes them an ideal platform for developing and deploying microservices.

A *container* is like a folder on your computer. It can hold files, but it doesn't have its own operating system. Containers share the same kernel as the host operating system, which makes them much lighter weight and faster than virtual machines. A virtual machine, by contrast, is like a computer within a computer. You can run an operating system inside of it and have complete control over that virtual machine.

The advantages of Docker include how:

- Docker enables you to create lightweight, self-contained containers for your applications. This helps you to improve performance and scalability.
- Docker helps you to automate the deployment of your applications. This helps you to speed up the process of deploying your applications and reduces the risk of errors.
- Docker enables you to run multiple isolated containers on a single host machine. This helps you to improve resource utilization and reduce costs.

A *Docker image* is a lightweight, portable, and reproducible operating system built with your application and all its dependencies.

A *Dockerfile* is a text file that contains all the commands you need to build a particular image. To create an image from scratch, you can start with a blank Dockerfile and add commands one at a time. This is a simple Dockerfile for provisioning an Apache webserver on Ubuntu 20.04:

```
FROM ubuntu:20.04
ENV DEBIAN_FRONTEND="noninteractive" TZ="America/Chicago"
RUN apt-get update
RUN apt-get install -y apache2
ADD index.html /var/www/html/
CMD /usr/sbin/apache2ctl -D FOREGROUND
EXPOSE 80
```

Alternately, you can clone an existing image and modify it to create your own custom image.

How is data stored in Docker containers? When you create an image or container, Docker creates a writable layer on top of the underlying layers. Any changes to the image or container are written to this layer, and the changes are not permanent until you commit them. If you delete an image or container, Docker reclaims the underlying layers.

Docker uses the Linux bridge mechanism to create a virtual network interface. When you start a Docker container, Docker creates a virtual network interface on the host, and bridges it to the container's virtual network interface. All containers on the same host are then connected to each other using this virtual network.

All major public cloud servers provide built-in integration for Docker containers, making them an excellent choice for many configuration automation workloads.

Since we're talking about container management tools, I should mention HashiCorp Packer. Packer is a tool for creating identical machine images for multiple platforms from a single source configuration. Packer is lightweight, portable, and efficient. It automates the creation of machine images by aggregating the output of various provisioning tools into a single image.

Unlike Docker, however, Packer cannot manage the full lifecycle of the containers it creates.

The preferred and dominant environment for running and, in some cases, even managing all of the tools we've already seen is Linux. The vast majority of physical and virtual servers currently active across the internet these days are running one distribution or another of Linus Torvald's open source operating system.

But that doesn't mean Microsoft's Windows Server isn't still a player. In the next section, we'll learn about the tool that's built primarily for Windows: DSC.

PowerShell DSC

DSC ("Desired State Configuration") is a PowerShell-based platform for automating the configuration of Windows-based systems. It enables you to declaratively specify the desired configuration state of target systems, and then have DSC apply that configuration automatically. DSC provides an efficient, reliable, and repeatable way to manage your systems.

PowerShell DSC is designed to be idempotent, meaning that it can be run multiple times without causing any adverse or unpredictable effects.

DSC can monitor the state of resources and report back any changes.

DSC is, as the name implies, built to take advantage of the PowerShell environment. You can therefore define and launch a workload from within PowerShell. Here's an example of a configuration from Microsoft documentation[1]:

[1]https://docs.microsoft.com/en-us/powershell/dsc/configurations/write-compile-apply-configuration?view=dsc-1.1&viewFallbackFrom=powershell-7.2

```
Configuration HelloWorld {

    # Import the module that contains the File resource.
    Import-DscResource -ModuleName PsDesiredStateConfigur\
ation

    # The Node statement specifies which targets to compi\
le MOF files for, when
    # this configuration is executed.
    Node 'localhost' {

        # The File resource can ensure the state of files\
, or copy them from a
        # source to a destination with persistent updates.
        File HelloWorld {
            DestinationPath = "C:\Temp\HelloWorld.txt"
            Ensure = "Present"
            Contents   = "Hello World from DSC!"
        }
    }
}
```

You can then compile your configuration code into a `.mof` file using this command:

```
. C:\Scripts\HelloWorld.ps1
HelloWorld
```

You apply the configuration using:

```
Start-DscConfiguration -Path C:\Scripts\HelloWorld -Verbo\
se -Wait
```

That should deploy your workload. In our sample case, that would create a `HelloWorld.txt` file in the predefined file system location.

Choosing your tool

With those descriptions, I hope you're in a better position to make an intelligent and informed choice. As a visual summary that might make things a bit easier, here's a feature matrix:

Tool	Open Source?	Free Version?	Model	Method	Language
Puppet	Yes	Yes	Declarative	Pull	Ruby, DSL
Chef	Yes	Yes	Declarative	Pull	Ruby
Ansible	Yes	Yes	Both	Push	Python, YAML
SaltStack	Yes	Yes	Both	Both	Python
Terraform	Yes	Yes	Declarative	Push	
Docker	Yes	Yes	Declarative	Push	YAML
PowerShell DSC	No	Yes	Declarative	Pull	PowerShell

Tool Features

Platform-Specific Tools

The software configuration management tools we saw in the previous chapter were all good at building and managing application workloads. But, to one degree or another, they were all platform-agnostic. Which is to say, that they didn't necessarily have an opinion or preference about *where* their applications should be hosted and run.

In this chapter we'll explore some platform-specific tools that are designed to integrate your application code deeply into their own environments. We'll begin with the big cloud providers.

AWS Elastic Beanstalk

AWS Elastic Beanstalk is a Platform as a Service (PaaS) offered by Amazon Web Services. It enables developers to quickly deploy and manage applications in the AWS cloud. Elastic Beanstalk reduces the time necessary to create and manage applications by providing a fully managed platform with all the necessary infrastructure components already in place.

Applications deployed on Elastic Beanstalk are automatically scalable, meaning that they can grow or shrink in response to changing traffic demands. This eliminates the need for developers to worry about capacity planning and server management. Additionally, Elastic Beanstalk provides built-in support for popular web frameworks, including Ruby on Rails, PHP, Java SE, Node.js, and Python.

Elastic Beanstalk can deploy Docker environments using Dockerfile definitions or even remotely-hosted Docker images.

Elastic Beanstalk itself is free, but you will be billed based on the region where your workload is hosted, the type of instance it uses, and amount of data transferred.

AWS CloudFormation

AWS CloudFormation is a service that enables you to create and manage a collection of related AWS resources. With CloudFormation, you can use a template to describe the architecture of your system, and the AWS services that you want to use. You can then use the template to generate an AWS stack, which is a collection of resources that are deployed together.

An CloudFormation template is a JSON-formatted, text-based file that describes the resources required by an application or system. It includes information such as the name and type of the resource, its properties, and any associated dependencies.

Below is a heavily truncated example of the CloudFormation template for launching a LAMP server:

```
{
  "AWSTemplateFormatVersion" : "2010-09-09",

  "Parameters" : {

    "KeyName": {
      "Description" : "existing EC2 KeyPair for SSH acces\
s",
      "Type": "AWS::EC2::KeyPair::KeyName",
      "ConstraintDescription" : "an existing EC2 KeyPair."
    },

    "DBName": {
      "Default": "MyDatabase",
```

```
        "Description" : "MySQL database name",
        "Type": "String",
        "MinLength": "1",
        "MaxLength": "64",
        "AllowedPattern" : "[a-zA-Z][a-zA-Z0-9]*",
        "ConstraintDescription" : "contains only alphanumer\
ic characters."
      },

    "Mappings" : {
      "AWSInstanceType2Arch" : {
        "t1.micro"    : { "Arch" : "HVM64"  },
        "t2.nano"     : { "Arch" : "HVM64"  },
        "t2.micro"    : { "Arch" : "HVM64"  },
        "t2.small"    : { "Arch" : "HVM64"  }
      },

      "AWSInstanceType2NATArch" : {
        "t1.micro"    : { "Arch" : "NATHVM64"  },
        "t2.nano"     : { "Arch" : "NATHVM64"  },
        "t2.micro"    : { "Arch" : "NATHVM64"  }
      }
,
      "AWSRegionArch2AMI" : {
        "af-south-1"        : {"HVM64" : "ami-064cc455f8a1ef\
504", "HVMG2"},
        "ap-east-1"         : {"HVM64" : "ami-f85b1989", "HV\
MG2"},
        "ap-northeast-1"    : {"HVM64" : "ami-0b2c2a754d5b4d\
a22""}
      }

    },

    "Resources" : {
```

```

    "WebServerInstance": {
      "Type": "AWS::EC2::Instance",
      "Metadata" : {
        "AWS::CloudFormation::Init" : {
          "configSets" : {
            "InstallAndRun" : [ "Install", "Configure" ]
          },

          "Install" : {
            "packages" : {
              "yum" : {
                "mysql"        : [],
                "mysql-server" : [],
                "mysql-libs"   : [],
                "httpd"        : [],
                "php"          : [],
                "php-mysql"    : []
              }
            },


    "WebServerSecurityGroup" : {
      "Type" : "AWS::EC2::SecurityGroup",
      "Properties" : {
        "GroupDescription" : "Enable HTTP access via port\
 80",
        "SecurityGroupIngress" : [
          {"IpProtocol" : "tcp", "FromPort" : "80", "ToPo\
rt" : "80", \
          "CidrIp" : "0.0.0.0/0"},
        ]
      }
    }
  },
```

```

  "Outputs" : {
    "WebsiteURL" : {
      "Description" : "URL for newly created LAMP stack",
      "Value" : { "Fn::Join" : ["", ["http://", { "Fn::Ge\
tAtt" : \
      [ "WebServerInstance", "PublicDnsName" ]}]] }
    }
  }
}
```

Docker containers on AWS

AWS ECS is a container service that enables you to run containers on AWS. You can use ECS to launch and manage containers across a cluster of Amazon EC2 instances. With ECS, you need to provision and manage a instance server cluster to host your container deployment.

AWS EKS, by contrast, is a *managed* Kubernetes service that lets you deploy, manage, and scale containerized applications using Kubernetes. EKS accepts your application code and definitions and handles the actual container orchestration across AWS resources invisibly.

The Microsoft Azure Cloud

Azure provides a feature called Azure Resource Manager (ARM) that is the Azure equivalent of AWS CloudFormation. ARM allows you to create and manage your resources in an orderly way using templates.

The Azure equivalent of AWS Elastic Beanstalk is Azure App Service.

Google Cloud Platform (GCP)

There is no direct GCP equivalent to AWS Elastic Beanstalk. However, there are several options that may be suitable for deploying and managing applications on GCP, including Google Kubernetes Engine, App Engine Flexible Environment, and Compute Engine instances with Kubernetes.

Google Cloud Platform (GCP) does not have an equivalent of AWS CloudFormation.

Speaking of Google, they're the creators of, and major contributors to the Kubernetes container orchestration tool. We'll talk about that next.

Kubernetes

Kubernetes is a system for managing containerized applications. It is an open source platform that enables developers to quickly and easily create, deploy, and manage containerized applications at scale. Kubernetes was originally created by Google and is now maintained by the Cloud Native Computing Foundation (CNCF).

Kubernetes clusters can be deployed on-premises or in the cloud.

As a quick introduction, let's install the lightweight Kubernetes version, MicroK8s, on a Linux machine. All you'll need for this in-and-out exercise is a distribution with the Snaps package manager installed. This single command will install all the core services, libraries, and binaries necessary for small, proof-of-concept demos.

```
snap install microk8s --classic
```

Just to prove that the installation succeeded, ask the service to list all the nodes that are currently running. Of course, there won't be any of those yet.

```
sudo microk8s.kubectl get nodes
No resources found.
```

There will, however, be a single service with a private IP address associated with it:

```
sudo microk8s.kubectl get services
NAME          TYPE         CLUSTER-IP     EXTERNAL-IP   POR\
T(S)   AGE
kubernetes    ClusterIP    10.152.183.1   <none>        443\
/TCP   80s
```

Finally, you can enable the browser-based Kubernetes administration dashboard using this microk8s.enable command. The output you'll get will include extra instructions for displaying and using the authentication token you'll need to connect.

```
sudo microk8s.enable dns dashboard
Enabling DNS
Applying manifest
serviceaccount/coredns created
configmap/coredns created
[...]
```

Related Trends

Configuration management is a critical part of software development and operations, yet it can be difficult to keep up with the latest trends and technologies in the field. In this chapter, we will discuss some of the most important trends touching on configuration management, including DevOps, CI/CD, and cloud-based solutions.

DevOps is a term that has been around for a long time, but it has really taken off in recent years as organizations have sought to improve collaboration between developers and operations staff. The goal of DevOps is to reduce the "friction" between these two groups, so that they can work more effectively together and produce better results. One way to achieve this is by using Continuous Integration (CI) and Continuous Delivery (CD) tools and processes.

CI refers to the practice of automatically building and testing software code changes as they are checked into a source code repository. This helps to ensure that new code does not break existing functionality, and allows developers to get feedback on their changes quickly. CD refers to automating the process of releasing software changes into production environments. This can help speed up the deployment process and reduce the risk of errors.

Cloud-based solutions have also become increasingly popular in recent years, as organizations have sought ways to reduce costs or take advantage of new capabilities offered by cloud providers. Configuration management solutions that run in the cloud can provide benefits such as scalability, ease of use, and automation.

DevOps

Just what is DevOps?

DevOps is a software development practice that promotes collaboration between software developers and information technology (IT) professionals. The goal of DevOps is to improve the quality and speed of software delivery through the use of automation, measurement, and communication.

The practice aims to shorten the feedback loop between software developers and IT professionals through the use of tools that automate application deployment and monitoring. This allows for more rapid identification and resolution of problems, which in turn leads to improved quality and speed of software delivery.

Continuous Integration

Continuous integration is the process of integrating new code into a project on a continual basis. This helps ensure that the codebase remains stable and that bugs are caught and fixed as quickly as possible. Continuous integration can be implemented using a variety of tools.

Among those tools is Jenkins, a popular open source Continuous Integration (CI) tool used for automating the build process in software development teams. It allows developers to create Jenkins jobs that define how their code should be compiled, tested, and deployed. Jobs can be run on demand or automatically triggered when changes are made to code repositories.

Travis CI is a Continuous Integration (CI) service used to build and test software projects hosted on GitHub. Travis CI integrates with GitHub repositories to provide automated builds and tests for projects as soon as new code is committed. In addition to automated builds, Travis CI can also be used to deploy projects to web servers or other destinations.

Continuous Delivery

Continuous Delivery (CD) is a software engineering practice that enables developers to release software in a more automated and reliable way. It helps reduce the risk of releasing new features by allowing developers to test them in a controlled environment before they are released to customers. CD also enables teams to ship software more frequently, which can lead to increased customer satisfaction and loyalty.

In order to achieve continuous delivery, you need to have a robust process in place that automates the build, testing, and deployment of your software. This process typically starts with code being checked into a source control repository, where it is then built and tested. Once the code has been verified as being good quality, it can be automatically released into a production environment.

There are many benefits of Continuous Delivery, including:

- Reduced risk when releasing new features - Automated testing ensures that new features are working correctly before they are released to customers
- Increased customer satisfaction and loyalty - Frequent releases can keep customers engaged and happy
- Improved team productivity - Automated processes allow team members to focus on tasks that add value rather than on menial tasks

CI and CD work together to ensure that code is always in a releasable state. CI checks in code and verifies that it meets the quality standards for the project. CD then takes that code and puts it into a release pipeline, where it is tested and deployed to production.

Cloud integration

CI and CD can be integrated with cloud platforms in a few ways. One option is to use a cloud-based CI/CD tool, such as Travis CI or CircleCI. These services allow you to automatically run your build and deployment processes on remote servers that are hosted by the service provider. This can be a convenient option if you don't have the resources to set up and manage your own CI/CD server infrastructure.

Another option is to use a cloud-based version of your application's runtime environment. For example, you could run your web application on Amazon Web Services (AWS) using an AWS Elastic Beanstalk environment. This would give you the ability to quickly deploy your application in a cloud-based environment, without needing to set up and manage your own servers.

As we've seen, Terraform is particularly well suited to cloud integration - even for workloads that span multiple clouds (i.e., AWS *and* Azure *and* GCP).

In addition, platforms like VMware provide tools like VMware Cloud on AWS for extending your local server infrastructure to the cloud, permitting integrated administration and monitoring.

Next Steps

Software Configuration Management (SCM) is a process that helps developers and organizations manage and control changes to software. By implementing a SCM process, you can ensure that changes are made in a controlled and safe manner, minimizing the risk of introducing errors into the software.

This book was an introduction to the concepts and tools you'll need to master if you decide to implement SCM within your own infrastructure. Whether you are just starting out with SCM or you are looking for new techniques and solutions, I hope this book has given you food for thought.

The next stop in your journey might involve choosing two or three of the technologies we've introduced here and trying them out for yourself. The more time you spend actually doing this stuff, they faster you'll master it.

Whatever your next steps, I hope you experience success and satisfaction

Good luck!

Made in the USA
Monee, IL
04 November 2026

67402827R00020

Where should we even begin?

Provisioning and configuring multiple remote servers and maintaining regular application updates is a challenge. Actually, it's many tough challenges, one on top of the other. As complexity increases and the pace of change builds, your only hope is some kind of automated orchestration.

You're certainly not the first person to notice the problem. There are, in fact, so many solutions out there that finding and implementing the *right* one is a job all on its own.

This short book will introduce you to the basics of software configuration management and provide you with the information you need to get started. Before long, you'll be applying the benefits of infrastructure automation to your own workflows. You'll learn about:

* Key tools like Puppet, Ansible, and Terraform
* Related trends like CI/CD and DevOps
* Integrations with major cloud platforms like AWS and Azure

ISBN 9781777721039

90000

9 781777 721039

OVERCOMING OBESITY

Foreword by
CHET P. HEWITT

COVERING THE ROADMAP TO YOUR SWEETEST VICTORY

BY AMOS NUGENT III